shot. Five months later King Charles I was beheaded at Whitehall in London.

The siege was a major blow to the Royalist cause and a disaster for the townspeople of Colchester.

Despite their own beliefs, the townspeople suffered at the hands of both sides. Lives and businesses were destroyed. By the end of the siege people had been reduced to eating dogs, cats and even rats to stay alive.

BELOW **Tending the wounded. A scene that would have been typical in the Parliamentarian siege camps around Colchester in the summer of 1648**

Painting by Robert Walker, 1649

Oliver Cromwell (1599–1658)

Oliver Cromwell was a wealthy landowner in Huntingdon. He was MP for Huntingdon and later for Cambridge. Like King Charles, he was devoted to his family and was a good huntsman. However, he was a Puritan. Puritans believed in a simpler way of worshipping God, without ceremony. Cromwell also believed in freedom of worship for all Protestants.

During the Civil War he was a brilliant cavalry commander and never lost a battle. After the fighting of 1648 he was a key figure in the decision to execute King Charles. When Thomas, Lord Fairfax retired in 1650, Cromwell finally accepted the role of commander-in-chief of the Parliamentarian army.

From 1653 until his death he governed England as Lord Protector. Neither Cromwell nor Charles was involved directly in the Siege of Colchester, but the outcome was crucial to both of them.

Why England Went to War with Itself

RIGHT **John Hampden, MP. He opposed Charles I over the 'ship-money' tax and was killed early in the Civil War**

BELOW **William Laud, appointed by Charles I as Archbishop of Canterbury in 1633. He was executed by Parliament in 1645**

RIGHT **Thomas Wentworth, 1st Earl of Strafford and adviser to Charles I. He was executed by Parliament in 1641**

RIGHT **Queen Henrietta Maria, Charles I's French wife, was disliked by many Puritans because she was Catholic**

Painting by Robert Walker

The underlying causes of the Civil War were money, religion and the balance of power between King Charles I and his Parliaments.

Parliament was different from today's. It contained all the wealthy landowners in England but had little power because the King ruled the country directly. One of Parliament's main functions was to raise money for the King. Charles I was often in need of money due to inflation, expensive wars against the French and Spanish and his lavish lifestyle.

Charles was out of touch with his people. This was particularly obvious in his attitude towards religion. Many people, both rich and poor, were Puritans who were unhappy with the Church of England, but Charles refused to allow other forms of worship.

Charles called his first Parliaments in the 1620s. He asked them to raise money for him, but the MPs argued with him over religion and foreign policy and refused. So from 1629 he tried to rule without Parliament, but his way of ruling was not popular.

In his desperation for money, he raked up long-forgotten

taxes, which he could raise without calling Parliament. The tax that caused most outrage was called 'ship-money'. John Hampden, who had earlier clashed with Charles in Parliament, objected to paying ship-money and took his case to court. Hampden lost in 1638, but only on a split decision of the judges. Throughout England he was seen as the moral victor.

A year earlier, in 1637, Charles' religious policy had reached a crisis. He had tried to force the Scots to accept the Church of England prayer book. They rebelled at this attempt to curb their style of worship. In 1640 Charles marched into Scotland, but he was decisively beaten. The Scottish army occupied Newcastle and demanded compensation from Charles. His only option was to call Parliament, which he did in November 1640.

This Parliament became known as the Long Parliament as it was not dissolved until after the end of the Civil War. John Pym, a wily Puritan, was the leading figure in Parliament. He carefully manipulated propaganda and events to reduce Charles' power and make him

A Civil W

Royalist victories are shown in red type,
Parliamentarian in blue

| 8 August 1642 Charles I declares war on Parliament | 23 October 1642 Battle of Edgehill | 13 July 1643 Battle of Roundway Down | Aug–Sept 1643 Siege of Gloucester, city holds out | 20 September 1643 1st Battle of Newbury | March 1644 1st Siege of Newark, town holds out |

Introduction

King Charles I (1601–49)
Charles Stuart became King in 1625. He was a small, shy and private man who, when he was young, suffered from a stammer. Only his wife, the French Catholic princess Henrietta Maria, and his family were ever close to him. He loved collecting art and hunting.

The war was the result of Charles' stubbornness. There were two main issues. He believed he was chosen by God to rule the country, without consulting Parliament, and he was at the centre of arguments about religion. King Charles was suspected of trying to make the Church of England more like the Roman Catholic Church.

Throughout the Civil War, Charles believed he would win because God had chosen him, but in the end his arrogance and scheming convinced the Parliamentarian army leaders that he could never be trusted. He was put through a show trial and executed. Even at the end Charles never accepted he was wrong. After his death many people regarded him as a martyr.

The Siege of Colchester in 1648 was one of the most important events of the English Civil War. A Royalist army, gathered from Kent, Hertfordshire and Essex, occupied Colchester. They were supporting King Charles I against Parliament. Once inside Colchester's walls, they were surrounded by the Parliamentarian army commanded by Thomas, Lord Fairfax.

The siege lasted seventy-six days during the summer of 1648. It was one of the coldest and wettest summers ever known. The siege ended with the surrender of the Royalists on 28 August. Two of the main Royalist leaders, Sir Charles Lucas and Sir George Lisle, were

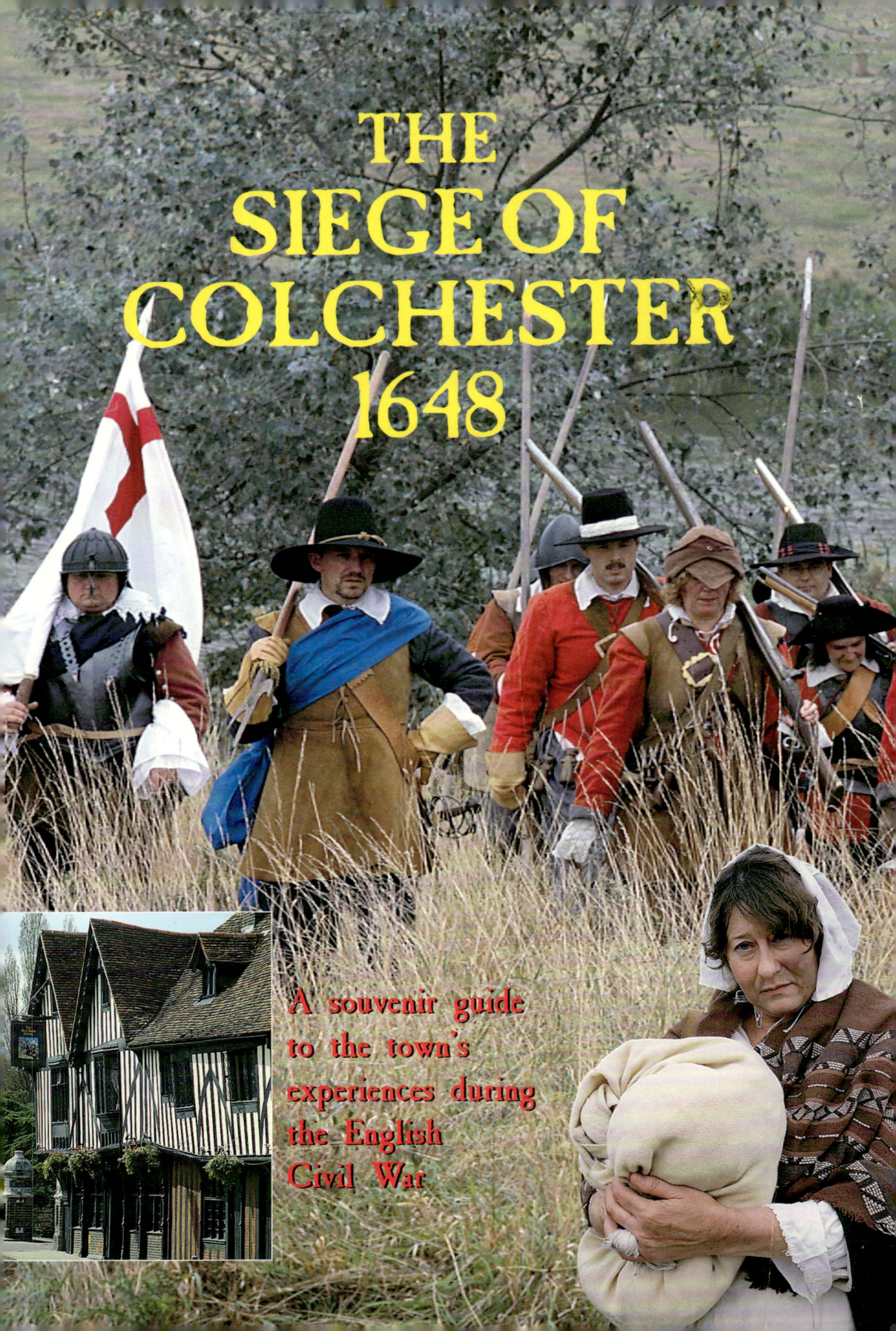

THE SIEGE OF COLCHESTER
1648

A souvenir guide
to the town's
experiences during
the English
Civil War

war became increasingly likely. Sides were taken largely on religious grounds, the strict Puritans being for Parliament, while the Church of England supported the King. The majority of people were faced with a hard choice. On 22 August King Charles raised the royal standard at Nottingham; the Civil War had started.

Painting by Samuel Cooper

LEFT **Charles I felt that God had given him his right to rule and that Parliament should not oppose him. Illustration from the *Eikon Basilike*, a Royalist book**

LEFT **John Pym, MP. Pym was Charles I's chief opponent in Parliament**

CENTRE BELOW **Robert Devereux, 3rd Earl of Essex, Parliamentarian commander-in-chief at the start of the Civil War**

obedient to Parliament.

In 1641 Pym listed all the examples of King Charles' misgovernment in a document called the Grand Remonstrance. This was narrowly approved by Parliament, but for many MPs it was a step too far. Parliament was now split.

On 4 January 1642 Charles decided to act against his enemies and tried, in person, to arrest five of them in Parliament, including Pym and Hampden. They escaped, and Charles was forced to leave London. Over the next few months, despite attempts at reconciliation,

Diary of the War until 1646

The first battle was fought at Edgehill in Warwickshire on 23 October 1642 and ended in a narrow Royalist victory, certainly not enough to end the war. The Royalists tried to take London but never succeeded, so Charles established his capital at Oxford. Throughout 1643 and early 1644 fortunes swayed either way as small armies grappled with each other in battles and sieges up and down the country.

However, on 2 July 1644 two Parliamentary and one Scots army combined to destroy the Royalist forces in northern England at Marston Moor, near York; the balance of power was tipping towards Parliament. On 14 June 1645 the recently formed New Model Army crushed Charles' army in the Midlands at Naseby. Small Royalist armies held on into 1646, but on 5 May Charles surrendered at Newark.

The war seemed to be over but there was more fighting to come.

LEFT *The Retreat at Naseby* by W. Giller from a painting by A. Cooper

| 2 July 1644 Battle of Marston Moor | 4 April 1645 Formation of New Model Army | 14 June 1645 Battle of Naseby | 5 May 1646 Charles I surrenders at Newark | June–August 1648 Siege of Colchester, town captured | 30 January 1649 Execution of Charles I |

The Way of War

RIGHT Women travelled with the armies helping to feed, clothe and nurse the soldiers

When the Civil War broke out, there was no one alive who had ever fought in a battle in England. Wartime experience was needed by both sides and this came from officers, such as Prince Rupert and Sir William Waller, who had fought in Holland and Germany.

Towns still had their medieval walls and castles, and fortified manor-houses dotted the country-side. Towns were often besieged during the war but a siege usually lasted only a few days. Typically, an attacking commander would demand that the defenders surrender. If they refused, cannon would be used to break down the town or castle walls. If a town was strongly defended, such as Gloucester and Newark, the siege could last a long

time. The attacking army would try to starve the defenders into submission by cutting off their supply of food. Defenders hoped that a friendly army nearby would come to their rescue. However, if this failed, under the rules of war they could expect little mercy.

For most of the Civil War there were a number of armies on both sides. Confusion ruled. They fought battles without a master plan. There was little discipline, and armies had many different styles and standards of uniforms.

Parliament decided to tackle this problem in its own forces. The New Model Army was formed on 4 April 1645 with Sir Thomas Fairfax as commander-in-chief and Oliver Cromwell as second in command. The New Model Army started to bring standards and discipline and was the first professional army in England. Previously, there was little to distinguish a Roundhead (Parliamentarian) from a Cavalier (Royalist). They wore the same clothing and armour and carried the same

CENTRE Shot for a type of small cannon known as a 'rabonett', found under the floor of a barn near Colchester

BELOW The New Model Army, created in 1645, was better armed, organised and disciplined than the Royalist troops that it faced

Load

types of weapons. It was not unknown in the heat of battle for a soldier to mistake the enemy for his own side. The slight differences were in the design of flag and colour of sash and coat worn by individual regiments.

At the start of the Civil War some armour and weapons that had last seen action over a century before were dusted off. Most soldiers wore only breast and backplates and a helmet. Musketeers normally wore no armour at all, preferring a broad-brimmed hat and coat in regimental colour. The cavalry wore a buff coat of leather under their armour, which was strong enough to resist many blows.

The lack of modern medicines meant that being wounded was often worse than being killed outright. Many of the injured would die slowly from infected wounds.

Swords were carried by officers and soldiers alike. Pikemen carried pikes, which were poles up to 18 feet (5.5m) long with a spearhead. In the rush to fight, even farmers' scythes and billhooks were used as weapons. Most of the foot-soldiers were armed with muskets, an early type of gun that was little more than an iron tube. The best musketeers could manage three shots a minute and could only hope to be accurate at up to 50 yards (46m).

Cannons came in many sizes, the heaviest being used only at sieges. We know that the Royalist gunner who occupied St Mary's Church tower had a cannon called a 'saker', which fired a $5\frac{1}{4}$lb (2.4kg) shot, and that the Parliamentarians shot back with two 'demi-cannon' and two 'culverins', firing 27lb (12.3kg) and 15lb (6.8kg) shot. Evidence of this damage on the tower can still be seen today. The top of the original church tower has been rebuilt in red brick.

LEFT Pikemen fought as a close-packed unit and tried to push their opponents off the battlefield

ABOVE An officer of the Essex Militia, who sided with Parliament

LEFT A sergeant armed with a sword and a partisan, his badge of rank

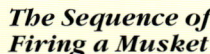

Aim   **Fire!**

The Sequence of Firing a Musket

The best musketeer could manage only three shots a minute with these primitive, but still deadly, guns

Colchester in the 1640s

There was general unrest in England during the reign of Charles I. Colchester had its share of troubles. The town is only 50 miles (80km) north of London and so news of the arguments between King and Parliament spread quickly. Cloth production was the major industry in the town, and the frequent slumps in demand caused widespread hardship and anger. Travelling preachers and foreigners arriving in the port at the Hythe spread extreme Puritan ideas, which caused most Colcestrians to support Parliament against the King.

The mix of religion, politics and poverty was powerful and explosive. Colchester had a reputation for being a divided and argumentative town. The leading political figures were constantly under attack.

The town was Parliamentarian but Parliament was resented for its heavy taxes on the town to pay for the army during the early years of the Civil War.

The Lucas family of St John's Abbey were powerful local landowners and had long quarrelled with most of the townspeople. In August 1642 Sir John Lucas was planning to join his brother, Sir Charles Lucas, in the Royalist army. The townspeople heard of this, and a huge crowd broke into his house. They seized armour and weapons and then went on to smash the family tombs in St Giles' Church. Sir John and his family were imprisoned in the Moot Hall and were only rescued by Sir Harbottle Grimston, the town's MP.

The unsettled conditions in Colchester allowed Matthew Hopkins, the self-styled 'Witchfinder General' to use the castle as a base in 1645. The town authorities were too busy fighting amongst themselves to worry about his activities. In May 1648 the Essex Trained Band, the local military force, had to be called in to deal with riots. Little did anyone know that within a few weeks the town would be at the centre of the Civil War.

Royalist Uprising

On 5 May 1646 King Charles I had surrendered, and the Civil War seemed over. However, he was still King and he had support.

In Kent there was growing resentment at the rule of Parliament. The Puritan Mayor of Canterbury tried to ban the celebration of Christmas in 1647. This caused riots, which die-hard Royalists used to stir up an open revolt. In May 1648 a new Royalist army was formed, led by Lord Goring, the old Earl of Norwich. Though he had little experience of fighting, Goring was soon joined by such veteran commanders as Sir George Lisle.

Sir Thomas Fairfax, now Lord Fairfax, gathered his soldiers of the New Model Army to meet the Royalist threat. He marched into Kent and defeated the Royalists at Maidstone on 1 June. Goring marched towards London, but at Blackheath he realised that London was not going to support the Royalist cause and so he crossed the Thames into Essex.

Here the Royalists attracted more support, including Lord Capel, who had looked after the royal children, and Sir Charles Lucas, who had ridden south from Colchester. At Chelmsford they surprised the County Committee of Parliament and took its members captive. However, they missed Sir Thomas Honywood of Marks Hall, who raised most of the Essex militia to fight the Royalists.

By now Fairfax had crossed to Essex, and the Royalists moved north, pausing to raid Leez Priory, the home of the Parliamentarian admiral, the Earl of Warwick.

On the morning of 12 June, about 4,000 Royalist soldiers arrived at Colchester. The townspeople tried to stop them but, faced by such a large force, the mayor reluctantly agreed to let them in. He threw the keys to the town over the wall so that he would not have to open the gate in person.

The Royalists expected to stay for a few days in Colchester, gathering strength and supplies for their army. However, Fairfax, hot on their heels, arrived the next day and immediately ordered the town to surrender. Goring refused, and at this Fairfax launched an attack on the Headgate, hoping to storm the town. After a pitched battle the Parliamentarians were beaten back, and a siege became the only option.

ABOVE **Sir Thomas Fairfax, commander-in-chief of the Parliamentarian New Model Army**

CENTRE TOP **Leez Priory, raided by the Royalists**

CENTRE MIDDLE **An account of the Royalist uprising**

CENTRE BOTTOM **Sir Thomas Honywood, Parliamentarian commander of the Essex Militia**

ABOVE **Royalist Sir William Campion was killed in the fighting at Headgate**

LEFT **Royalist defenders fought off the Parliamentarians' attempt to storm Colchester**

The Siege Begins

RIGHT AND CENTRE **Clay-pipes and an entrenching tool from the site of Colonel Ewer's fort**

BELOW **Colonel Rainsborough, the Parliamentarian siege expert**

RIGHT **An account of the fight at Headgate**

BELOW RIGHT **Pottery from the site of Colonel Ewer's fort**

RIGHT **The siege quickly developed into a waiting game**

Fairfax established his headquarters in Lexden and set about closing Colchester off from the outside world. He realised that the Royalists could be supplied by sea, so he seized the fort at East Mersea, which guarded the Colne estuary. Parliament sent Colonel Rainsborough, a noted expert on siege warfare, to advise Lord Fairfax on further measures.

A series of forts and trenches were built all round the town. These were probably banks of earth surrounded by ditches and fences. The forts were later used as platforms for forty heavy cannons sent from the Tower of London. The forts were named after their commanders.

An excavation in the 1920s on the site of Colonel Ewer's fort found clay-pipes smoked by the soldiers. Musket-balls, gunpowder measures and fragments of windows were also found. The lead from the windows would have been melted down into bullets. All these can be seen today in the Castle Museum.

Sir Charles Lucas, who was one of the best cavalry commanders during the Civil War and also a local man, became the real leader of the Royalists. He started to make arrangements to resist a siege. Parts of the town wall were strengthened. Luckily for the Royalists, large stores of corn, wine, salt, fish and gunpowder were found at the Hythe. Raiding parties were sent out to disrupt the work on the forts and to capture more supplies of food.

In mid-June, a request for an exchange of prisoners was refused by Fairfax. The Royalists also wrecked attempts to end the siege. They demanded too much from the peace negotiations conducted by the Parliamentary Committee members they had captured. The siege was set to continue.

The East Street Sortie

Towards the end of June the Parliamentarians brought in forces from Suffolk to close off routes to the north. Sir Harbottle Grimston's house by Lexden Road, in which Royalist snipers were hiding, was destroyed. Colonel Whalley took Greenstead church and set up a gun battery in the churchyard, cutting off escape to the east. On 5 July the Parliamentarians moved forward to occupy the mill at East Bridge.

This last move was too much for Sir Charles Lucas. It cut off the route used by many Royalist raiding parties searching for food and also threatened the Hythe. That very night 500 foot-soldiers, led by Sir George Lisle, and 200 horsemen, commanded by Lucas, charged down East Hill.

Arriving at the East Bridge they met Parliamentarian musketeers, and a sharp fight took place in which many of the musketeers were killed. Today the house known as the Siege House, overlooking East Bridge, still shows a wall pitted with lead bullets.

The Royalist infantry stormed across the river and hurled one of the Parliamentarian guns into the river. Lucas' cavalry chased the Parliamentarian troops along East Street and on to the hill by the Harwich Road. Here Colonel Whalley had drawn up his men from the Greenstead battery to stop the Royalists.

A pitched battle took place. The crucial moment was when one of Whalley's soldiers heard a Royalist shout for more ammunition and realised that they were running short. This gave the Parliamentarians fresh energy, and Colonel Whalley's cavalry launched a fierce counter-attack.

The Royalists were forced back into the town. They had killed many Parliamentarians and taken prisoners, but they had lost soldiers themselves and had collected no food. Only a day later the Parliamentarians reoccupied East Street and began to burn houses at the foot of East Hill.

ABOVE **Greenstead church, used as a Parliamentarian fort**

LEFT **Cavalry equipment from the site of Colonel Ewer's fort**

BELOW **A musket-ball embedded in a window from the Siege House**

ABOVE **The Royalist commander, Sir George Lisle**

LEFT **The Siege House still bears the marks of battle**

Siege Landmarks

*St Martin's Church –
tower destroyed
during Siege*
1

*The King's Head (now a
solicitors' office) –
Royalist officers held here*
11

*St Mary at the Walls –
top of tower blown off by
Parliamentarians*
10

The Siege of
COLCHESTER
by the Lord Fairfax as it was
with the Line & Outworks,
1648.

*St John's Abbey Gate –
badly damaged in
massive explosion*
9

*St Giles' Church –
contains Lucas
family tombs*
8

Castle – Lucas and Lisle held here before execution
2

Greenstead Church – site of a Parliamentarian fort
3

A: St. Martins
B: St. Rumbals
C: St. Tenants Chap.
D: St. Nicholas
E: Allhallows
F: St. James
G: St. Botolphs
H: St. Gyles's

I: North Gate
K: East Gate
L: Boroughs &
M: Shore Gate
N: Head Gate
O: High Street
P: East Street
Q: Borough St:
L: St. Marys

R: Wyer Street
S: Cow Street
T: Middleboro
V: Bouchers
W: More Elm La
W: Trinity Lane
X: St. Martins La.
Y: Tenants Lane

The Siege House – Royalist musket-ball holes in beams
4

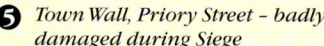

Town Wall, Priory Street – badly damaged during Siege
5

6
St Leonard's at the Hythe – Royalist loopholes in door

7
St Botolph's Priory – destroyed during Siege

The Capture of St John's Abbey Gate

On 14 July, Colonel Whalley took advantage of the Parliamentarians' strong position on the east side of Colchester by closing in on the port at the Hythe.

Though the St Leonard's Church at the Hythe had been prepared to withstand an attack, it was surrendered to Whalley's men with little resistance. All the supplies from the warehouses at the Hythe had been taken earlier by the Royalists, so there was now little point in defending the church. Holes can still be seen in the door, which were probably made from within for use as loopholes by Royalist musketeers.

On the same day, Fairfax used the heavy cannon he had recently received from London to attack the Lucas family home, St John's Abbey. After a day-long bombardment the Parliamentarians managed to storm the house, clearing it room by room in vicious hand-to-hand fighting.

The surviving Royalists took refuge in the strongpoint of St John's Abbey gateway. Eventually a Parliamentarian grenade landed in the Royalist gunpowder store. The roof of the gateway was blown off in a deafening explosion. The Royalists set fire to the nearby houses as they retreated into the town. This stopped them from being used as Parliamentarian gunplatforms for firing over the walls.

The Parliamentarian troops, still hot-tempered from the recent fighting, found little to loot in the house so they went on to St Giles' Church, which contained the Lucas family tombs. The bodies of Elizabeth Lucas, Sir Charles Lucas' mother,

and another relative, both of whom had been buried only a year before, were pulled out of their coffins and ripped to pieces. Some of the soldiers wore locks of Lucas hair in their hats.

This was the worst of a number of crimes of which both sides were accused in a propaganda war. Royalists were thought to use poisoned and chewed bullets to inflict horrific wounds. Parliamentarians were suspected of murdering townspeople in their beds. Sir Charles Lucas was accused of rape.

The capture of St John's Abbey allowed Fairfax to remove a thorn in his side. In the Church of St Mary-at-the-Walls was a one-eyed Royalist gunner who had a small cannon known as a saker. With this he caused havoc among Fairfax's troops, especially when they were building the forts on the west side of the town.

For some time all efforts to remove this sniper had failed. But now, after the capture of St John's Abbey, Fairfax was able to position heavy cannons on St John's Green and destroy the top of the tower, killing the gunner.

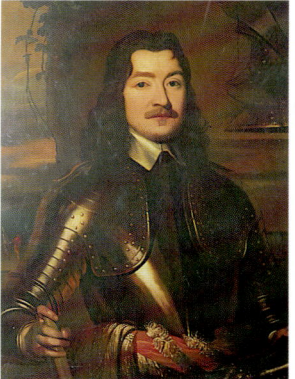

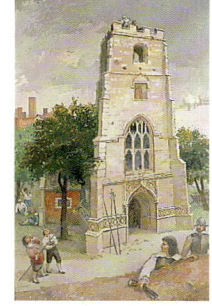

ABOVE A one-eyed Royalist gunner fired from the tower of St Mary at the Walls

LEFT Sir Charles Lucas was the main Royalist commander and a Colchester man

BELOW Leaflets, printed in London, were used to spread both Parliamentarian and Royalist propaganda

5 Julii, 11 at night.
A
LETTER
From the Leaguer before
Colchester,
Sent to the Honorable Committee at DERBY House,
OF
The great Fight between his Excellency
The Lord FAIRFAX,
AND
The Forces in Colchester.

Ordered by the said Committee, That this Letter be forthwith Printed and Published.
GUALTHER FROST Secr'

London, Printed for Edward Husband, Printer to the Honorable House of Commons, July 7. 1648.

6. Julii, 1648.
From the
LEAGUER
AT
Colchester,
…ore certain News of the
…IGHT
on Wednesday last;
AND
…eir present condition.

PRinted by the Appointment of the Honorable Committee at De…
GUALT…

London, Printed for Edward Hu… …norable House of Comm…

A Flaming
BULL
From
COLCHESTER

Most judicious and loyall Reader,

HAving received severall dictations from the various faces of severall Personages, touching the new found stratagems of the besieged Royalists in the Town of Colchester, I thought it requisit to present to your view, the marrow and foundation, from whence it did precede, viz. Sir Charles Lucas, and the rest of his distressed brethren, having had severall consultations about their present afflictions and surrounding, began to bethink themselves of some miraculous stratagem (not doubting but that it would take effect) to release them from their immediate thraldom and

A
LETTER
SENT
To the Honorable William Lenthal Esq; Speaker of the Honorable House of Commons,
Of the late
Fight at Colchester,
AND,
How the Suburbs of the said Town were fired by
The Lord Goring, Lord Capel, Sir Charls Lucas, and the rest of the Enemy.

PRinted by the Command of the Honorable William Lenthal Esq; Speaker of the Honorable House of Commons.

London, Printed for Edward Husband, Printer to the Honorable House of Commons, July 17. 1648.

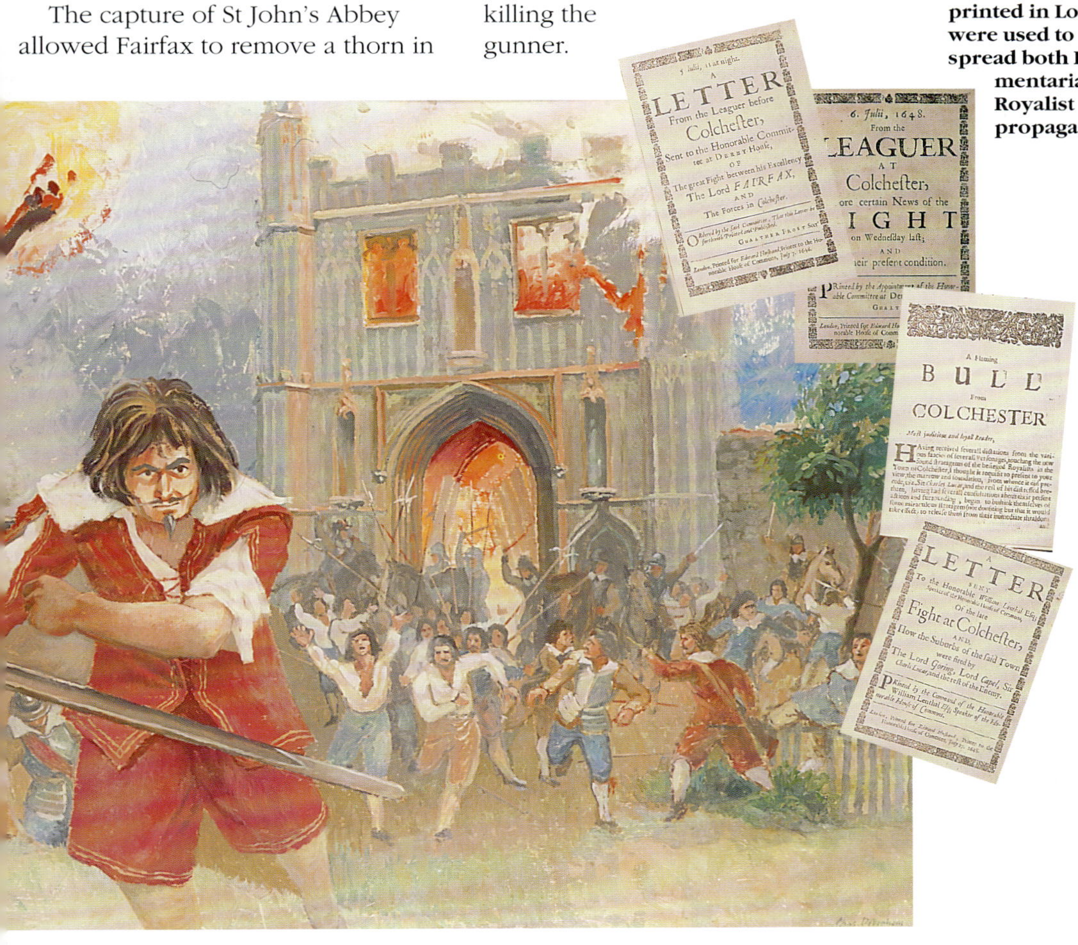

'Colchester's Teares'

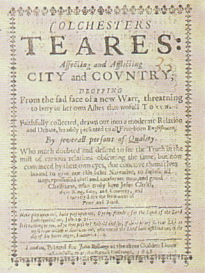

Conditions within the town were getting worse. Food was scarce; butter and cheese were selling at high prices. The townspeople not only had to find room to house Royalist soldiers but also lost the thatch from their roofs to feed their horses. The weather had turned cold and wet at the start of the siege and remained this way almost until the end, so adding to the suffering.

In late July the cavalry were ordered to hand over every third horse for meat to feed the Royalist soldiers. In an attempt to boost morale a whole horse was roasted at Headgate on 22 July, but this was just a gesture. By early August, despite a bloody sickness caused by maggot-ridden horse flesh, the stables were still being robbed at night and the meat sold by the pound. The soldiers were even eating dogs. An eyewitness report said that the soldiers used to keep back part of their bread ration to lure a dog close enough so that it could be clubbed to death. A side of small dog could sell for 6 shillings (over £15 today).

The soldiers were lucky compared to the townspeople who, in addition to dogs, were reduced to eating cats, rats and mice. Candles, made in those days mostly from mutton fat, were also eaten. However,

these last, pitiful sources of food were running out, and by the second week of August the townspeople were starving. They gathered each evening outside Lord Goring's house begging him to surrender. The men were clubbed off with muskets, but the women and children would not

RIGHT *An Incident at the Siege of Colchester* by Harry Becker shows the townspeople pleading with the Royalist soldiers

BELOW **By the end of the siege people were even eating rats and candles**

14

move and 'lay howling and crying on the ground for bread'. Sir Charles Lucas, as a local man, sympathised with them and demanded that they should be given some grain from the Royalists' store. This could only be a temporary measure.

Five days later these same desperate women and children came out of the town to throw themselves on the mercy of the Parliamentarian Colonel Rainsborough. But, far from helping them, Rainsborough threatened to strip some of the women naked if they did not immediately return to the town.

This was the townspeople's darkest hour during the siege. They had wanted to support Parliament in the first place but had been forced to fight for the Royalists. They were now receiving the worst from both sides. On 21 August a local doctor, Dr Glisson, tried to persuade Fairfax to allow some of the starving people to leave the town, but Fairfax refused. From his point of view, the more mouths to be fed inside Colchester the

quicker the town would fall.

Colchester itself now lay in ruins. Many homes were smashed and burnt. St Botolph's Priory, the town's main church, had been destroyed by both Parliamentarian and Royalist guns. The priory overlooked the town walls and so posed a great threat if it was captured and held by either side.

St Martin's Church, one of the oldest in the town, was bombarded from Fort Rainsborough, to the north of the town. The top of the tower came crashing down and was reduced to little more than a heap of rubble. Today, the tower is only a short stub, a tribute to the accuracy of the gunners who demolished it from a range of more than a mile (1.6km).

ABOVE Many townspeople lost their homes and belongings and had to scavenge for food

BELOW The Church of St Mary at the Walls lost the top of its tower and it remained ruined for sixty years after the siege

LEFT St Botolph's Priory was caught in the crossfire and was completely destroyed during the siege

The Surrender

ABOVE
Commissary General Ireton, one of the Parliamentarian commanders and the son-in-law of Oliver Cromwell

BELOW **Colonel Maxey, who is thought to have been among the Royalist cavalry who escaped from Colchester**

CENTRE **Leaflets giving news from Colchester towards the end of the siege**

BELOW **A smelly message sent to the Parliamentarians by die-hard Royalists!**

As July wore on, Fairfax's noose round the town pulled tighter. On 16 July he offered honourable surrender terms to the ordinary Royalist soldiers. Lord Goring and the other Royalist leaders were outraged at this attempt to undermine them. They threatened to hang any future Parliamentarian messenger who tried a similar tactic. An offer of an exchange of prisoners made by Fairfax was also rejected.

At the end of July the Royalists' hopes were raised when they learned that other troops around the country were rising to fight for King Charles. If they were successful, the Parliamentarians would be forced to lift their siege. The Earl of Holland, who had led a rising in the west, was quickly defeated and captured near London. However, the Duke of Hamilton, who had invaded from Scotland on behalf of the King, was still fighting. This encouraged the Royalists in Colchester to hold on.

Some of the Royalist cavalry managed to escape from Colchester on 22 July, but the Parliamentarians blocked this escape route by building another fort near Middle Mill. Further efforts to break out of the town were unsuccessful and, as August wore on, some of the Royalist troops began to desert. Fairfax encouraged this by offering them free passes to go to their homes if they would give up their weapons and leave the fight.

Fairfax knew that it was only a matter of time before the Royalists would be starved into surrender, so he refused all attempts by the Royalists to wriggle out of this fate. The townspeople became pawns in this battle of wills. Desperate for food, they pleaded with the Royalists to let them leave Colchester, but they were trapped.

On 22 August the Parliamentarians fired arrows into Colchester telling the Royalists that the Duke of Hamilton had been beaten by Oliver Cromwell at the Battle of Preston in Lancashire. One arrow was

fired back with a turd attached as 'an answer from Colchester as you may smell'. But this was a futile gesture as all hope of rescue had now gone. The Parliamentary Committee men who had been captured by the Royalists at Chelmsford and the local physician Dr Glisson tried to organise treaties to end the siege, but now the only terms that Fairfax would accept were unconditional surrender.

In a last, desperate gamble on 25 August the Royalist leaders secretly gathered their troops near a section of the town wall that had been reduced to rubble. They hoped to charge out and escape, but the soldiers were convinced that the officers only wanted to save themselves. They mutinied and, although they were eventually reassured, all hope of surprise was lost.

On 27 August the Royalist Colonel Tuke was to Fairfax's camp at the Hythe to receive the terms for the Royalist surrender. All remaining horses, arms, ammunition, colours (flags) and drums were to be surrendered. The ordinary soldiers and lower officers – about 3,500 survived – were to parade with their baggage at Greyfriars and were to receive 'fair quarter'. All lords and higher-ranking officers were to assemble at the King's Head (now a solicitors' office just off Head Street) to await the Parliamentarian 'mercy'.

On 28 August, eleven weeks after the siege had begun, Lord Fairfax's victorious Parliamentary troops entered the town.

ABOVE **The document of surrender that ended the Siege of Colchester**

BELOW **Dr Glisson, a Colchester physician, tried to negotiate an end to the siege**

LEFT **The Parliamentarian troops finally entered Colchester on 28 August 1648**

BELOW **The senior Royalist officers were held prisoner in the King's Head**

Retribution

If Fairfax had been forced to storm Colchester under the then terms of war, he could have let his soldiers steal all they wanted and butcher Royalists and townspeople alike. He did not let this happen but the outcome of surrender after such a long siege was still harsh. Fairfax ordered the townspeople to pay him the huge fine of £14,000 (well over £2 million in today's terms). The people objected; it was so obvious that most people had lost every-thing. So he reduced the sum, but only to £12,000, of which £2,000 was for relief of the poor. Half was paid by the wealthy Dutch and Flemish weavers, who would have to rely on a quick upturn in trade to avoid ruin.

The walls of the town were ordered to be knocked down so that nobody could ever fortify the town again. This job fell to the Parliamentarian Sir Thomas Honywood. Perhaps because he was a local man, he was slow to act. In the end, only the south-west section of the ancient wall was demolished.

Despite being offered 'fair quarter', the common soldiers, who could not afford to buy their freedom, had an extremely cruel fate. They were herded out of

Colchester, stripped of much of their clothing, beaten and half-starved. Many were even sent abroad as slaves to the West Indies.

Fairfax had stated that the Royalist officers surrendered 'at mercy'. This, in most cases, meant that their lives were spared and that they would later be able to buy their freedom. However, four were summoned from the King's Head to the Moot Hall, where Fairfax and his officers sat in judgement. Colonel Farr escaped through a window but Sir Charles Lucas, Sir George Lisle and

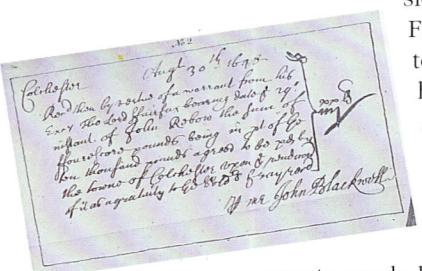

The manner of His Excellency Sir *Thomas Fairfax*, and the Officers of His Armie sitting in COVNCELL.

Sir Bernard Gascoigne were marched off.

Earlier in the Civil War, Lucas had been captured at the Battle of Stow-on-the-Wold, and Lisle at the Siege of Farringdon, near Oxford. Both had been freed on condition that they promised never to fight against Parliament again. This, of course, they had done, so when they became Fairfax's prisoners, he saw their lives as forfeit. He also wanted to make an example to show others what would happen if they continued to fight against Parliament.

Lucas and Lisle in their defence said that they thought the rising in 1648 was a different war so the promise did not count. They argued that the heavy fines they had paid to regain their estates made up for breaking their promise. The verdict, however, was unanimous. They were to be taken to the castle and executed that evening by firing squad.

As they prepared for death, one of the guards discovered that Sir Bernard Gascoigne was in fact an Italian soldier from Florence. He was determined to die as he had fought, alongside Lucas and Lisle. But the Parliamentarians decided to spare him as they did not want to damage relations with the Duke of Tuscany and risk the lives of any Parliamentarians who travelled to Italy.

Lucas and Lisle received no such reprieve. At 7 p.m. on Monday, 28 August 1648 they were led out to the north wall of the castle. After again questioning the legality of his execution, Lucas said a short prayer, faced the muskets and said: 'See, I am ready for you; and now, rebels, do your worst'. Sir George Lisle knelt and kissed his dead friend. He asked his executioners to come nearer, in case they missed him in the evening light. Tradition soon gave his last words as 'Shoot rebels; your shot, your shame; our fall, our fame'.

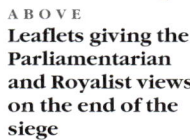

ABOVE Leaflets giving the Parliamentarian and Royalist views on the end of the siege

LEFT Sir Bernard Gascoigne, who was discovered to be an Italian soldier

BELOW Destruction of the town walls can be seen in Priory Street

BELOW The obelisk in the Castle Park marks the spot where Lucas and Lisle were shot

The Aftermath

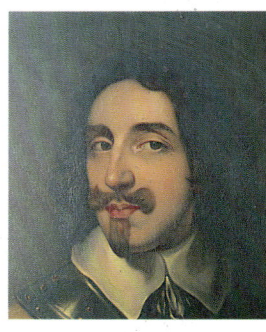

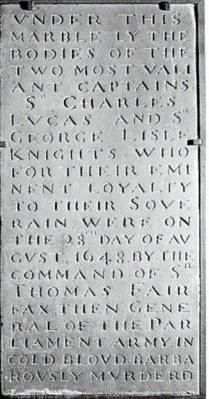

The Members of Parliament were angry that Fairfax had executed Lucas and Lisle without consulting them. They tried two of the other Royalist commanders. Lord Goring, the Earl of Norwich, was saved from death by the single vote of Speaker Lenthall, who had once borrowed money from him. Goring died of old age in his London home. He was one of the luckiest of the Royalist leaders.

Lord Capel was condemned to death by Parliament and shut up at Windsor Castle. He was then taken to the Tower of London, from where he escaped dramatically; he was one of the few prisoners who ever did so. But he was recaptured shortly afterwards and beheaded at Whitehall in March 1649.

King Charles I was seen by the New Model Army as the cause of all the bloodshed of 1648. Cromwell and his son-in-law Ireton, who had fought at the Siege of Colchester, were determined that King Charles should pay with his life. The army removed any opposition in Parliament, and the few remaining MPs brought Charles to trial on a charge of treason against his own people. Inevitably, he was found guilty and was executed at Whitehall on 30 January 1649. Fairfax refused to be a member of the court to try King Charles I. He became disillusioned with the way events were going and retired from the army shortly after the fall of Colchester. He lived his last years at Nun Appleton, his Yorkshire home. From here, Parliamentarian though he was, he helped to bring back King Charles II in 1660.

In 1669 Sir Bernard Gascoigne came back to Colchester with his master, the Duke of Tuscany, to visit the newly erected memorial to Lucas and Lisle in St Giles' Church and to point out the spot on which they had died.

By then the cloth trade had picked up, and Colchester was once again a thriving town. However, many buildings still lay ruined, and some damaged ones, such as St Mary's Church, were not repaired for another sixty years. The real damage though was to the townspeople who had lived through the shattering events of the siege and would have to carry their memories to the grave.

Further Information

Walking Tour

A walking tour with a qualified Blue Badge Guide can help you to discover more about the people and places associated with the Siege of Colchester. Just call the Colchester Visitor Information Centre on 01206 282920 for details. Alternatively, you can call in to the centre at 1 Queen Street (opposite the castle).

The Essex Militia

The Essex Militia is a re-enactment group which re-creates historical events and daily life in the period from 1600 to 1700. Typically, they perform at historic houses or in their own encampments. The Essex Militia also demonstrates military combat, sword displays and the firing of muskets and cannon. The Essex Militia can be contacted on 01277 655612.

David T-D. Clarke, *The Siege of Colchester 1648*
Taylor Downing and Maggie Millman, *Civil War* (1991)
Wilfrid Emberton, *The English Civil War Day by Day* (1995)
Jasper Ridley, *The Roundheads* (1976)
John Tincey, *Soldiers of the English Civil War, Vol. 2 Cavalry* (1990)
Peter Young, *The English Civil War Armies* (1973)

Reference copies of the these works may be consulted at the Museum Resource Centre, 14 Ryegate Road, Colchester (by appointment only, tel. 01206 282931), or in Colchester Central Library in Trinity Square.

Photograph Credits

Many of the photographs and illustrations used in this guide were taken from Colchester Museums' collection. In addition other photographs were taken by Neil Jinkerson and John Brooks of Jarrold Publishing and by Tony Kora. The picture of John Pym was provided by the Courtauld Institute of Art. The pictures of Charles I, Oliver Cromwell, John Hampden, William Laud, Thomas Wentworth, Henrietta Maria, Robert Devereux and the execution of Charles I are by courtesy of the National Portrait Gallery, London.

The kind permission of the following institutions to publish is also acknowledged: Essex Society for Archaeology and History (Eikon Basilike frontispiece and view of Colchester in 1669); Northampton Museums and Art Gallery (*The Retreat at Naseby*).

Special thanks go to the Essex Militia for their enthusiasm and help in illustrating this guide.

Acknowledgements

This guide was compiled by Tom Hodgson, Colchester Museums' Curator of Social History, using information from the following publications, whose authors are gratefully acknowledged:

David Appleby, *Our Fall Our Fame: The Life and Times of Sir Charles Lucas* (1996)
Maurice Ashley, *The English Civil War* (1990)
Stuart Asquith, *New Model Army 1645–60* (1981)
Mark Bence-Jones, *The Cavaliers* (1976)
R.E. Boustred, *Last Stand for the King* (1974)
Matthew Carter, *A True Relation of that ... Expedition of Kent, Essex and Colchester in 1648* (1789)

ISBN 0-7117-1029-5
© Colchester Borough Council and Jarrold Publishing 1998.
Designed and produced by Jarrold Publishing, Norwich.
Printed in Great Britain 1/98

THE
LOYALL
SACRIFICE.

Shoot

Rebells

your shott, your shame;
Our fall, our fame.

The execution of Lucas and Lisle, seen here as a martyrdom by
Royalists, but as justice by Parliamentarians

COLCHESTER

JARROLD
PUBLISHING

THE SIEGE OF
COLCHESTER 1648
Published in association with
Colchester Borough Council

ISBN 0-7117-1029-5

9 780711 710290